STAR WARS®

EARTH'S SOLAR SYSTEM

By Samantha Margles

Photographs © 2014:

Corbis Images/Science Photo Library: 31 bottom

European Southern Observatory: 4

European Space Agency (ESA): cover top right; 22 right (CNES/D. Ducros); 23 Saturn (Hubble Heritage Team/NASA)

Getty Images: cover center, 3 planets (Stocktrek Images); 6 & 7 (Stocktrek Images); 5 background (World Perspectives); 26 & 27 background (Chad Baker/Digital Vision); 30 & 31 background (Picture Press)

iStockphoto: cover (adventtr); cover top left (martin_adams); 23 Jupiter (martin_adams2000)

NASA: cover lower right; 5 foreground (M. Weiss//CXC/M/); 8 foreground, 10 foreground, 11 foreground, 13 moons, 14 foreground, 15 foreground, 23 Venus, 23 Neptune, 25 foreground (JPL); 21 Earth (Reto Stockli/Alan Nelson/Fritz Hasler); 22 Earth, 23 Earth; 23 Mercury (Johns Hopkins University Applied Physics Laboratory/Carnegie Institution of Washington); 23 Mars (JPL/USGS); 27 foreground (Johns Hopkins University Applied Physics Laboratory/Arizona State University/ Carnegie Institution of Washington. Image reproduced courtesy of Science/AAAS); 32 (JPL-Caltech/UCLA); 28, 29; 31 top (SOHO)

Science Source: 2 & 3 (NASA/CXC/JPL-CALTECH/ESA-STSCI); 9 foreground, 12 foreground, 13 foreground; 18 foreground, 19 foreground (European Space Agency/DLR/FU Berlin/G. Neukum); 22 left (Detlev van Ravenswaay); 23 Uranus (Mark Garlick); 23 Neptune; 24 foreground (Steve A. Munsinger)

Shutterstock, Inc.: cover (clearviewstock); 8 & 9 background, 10 & 11 background, 12 & 13 background, 14 & 15 background (clearviewstock); 19 center (Aaron Rutten); 21 background (solarseven); 24 & 25 background (Maria Starovoytova),

ISBN 978-0-545-58517-0

Published by Scholastic Inc., 557 Broadway, New York, NY 10012. Scholastic and associated logos are trademarks and/or registered trademarks of Scholastic Inc.

12 11 10 9 8 7 6 5 4 3 2 1   14 15 16 17 18 19/0

Printed in the U.S.A.   40

First printing, January 2014

SCHOLASTIC INC.

"It's time for a trip, Artoo," said C-3PO. R2-D2 and C-3PO are droids—that's another word for robots. They are best friends and have had many adventures together in a galaxy far, far away. . . .

Today, they've decided to explore where we live in their spaceship. "Look, it's the Milky Way Galaxy!" said C-3PO.

MILKY WAY GALAXY

THE CENTER OF THE MILKY WAY GALAXY, LOCATED 26,000 LIGHT YEARS FROM EARTH

R2-D2 made a series of funny beeping sounds. "That's right, Artoo," C-3PO said. "According to the ship's computer, the Milky Way is huge. It has more than two hundred billion stars. We can't fly near the center, though—there's a black hole there!"

SAGITTARIUS

THE BLACK HOLE AT THE CENTER OF THE MILKY WAY GALAXY

Black holes draw anything near them in—even light. This black hole has the gravity of four million suns.

BLACK HOLE

THE BLACK HOLE'S ENORMOUS GRAVITY STRETCHES THE STAR (ORANGE CIRCLE) UNTIL IT IS TORN APART.

THIS BLACK HOLE WILL DESTROY SHIPS THAT PASS TOO CLOSE. WE'RE DOOMED!...UNLESS WE GET OUT OF HERE!

As soon as the two friends moved away from the black hole, R2-D2 spotted a solar system to explore.

Jupiter

Mars

Earth

Venus

Mercury

Sun

SOLAR SYSTEM

THIS SOLAR SYSTEM FORMED
AROUND 4.6 BILLION YEARS AGO!

This is our solar system—it has eight true planets that all orbit around one sun.

Saturn

Uranus

Neptune

Pluto

BEEP-BEE-WOO.

NO, ARTOO. PLUTO IS **NOT** THE NINTH PLANET IN THIS SYSTEM. PLUTO IS A **DWARF PLANET**. THAT MEANS IT IS TOO SMALL TO BE A REAL PLANET, BUT TOO BIG TO BE A SATELLITE.

This blue planet is Neptune. It is the farthest planet from the sun, and can get as cold as -353°F.

BRRRR!
THAT'S COLDER THAN HOTH!

The next planet is Uranus. Colliding with another large object may have pushed it over so it rotates on its side.

The next planet is Saturn. Saturn has a thick outer layer of gas and only becomes solid deep down near the center.

SATURN HAS OVER SIXTY MOONS.

THE BIGGEST ONE IS TITAN—IT'S BIGGER THAN THE PLANET MERCURY!

BEEP-BOOP.

SATURN

THE RINGS AROUND THE PLANET ARE
MOSTLY ICE, AND THE STRIPES ARE GASES
BLOWN BY THE WIND.

Like Saturn, Jupiter is known as a gas giant—meaning a large planet made primarily of gas, rather than rock and solid matter.

Great Red Spot

SEE JUPITER'S GREAT RED SPOT? IT'S A WINDSTORM THAT'S THOUSANDS OF MILES ACROSS!

JUPITER

JUPITER IS THE LARGEST PLANET IN OUR SOLAR SYSTEM. IT IS SO BIG, IT COULD FIT 1,300 EARTHS INSIDE IT.

Jupiter has sixty-seven confirmed moons.
The moons are made up of different materials,
and many have their own names.

EUROPA

MADE OF ICE

IO

COVERED WITH VOLCANOES

SIXTY-SEVEN MOONS?
OH MY GOODNESS!

CALLISTO

ROCKY AND COVERED
WITH CRATERS

GANYMEDE

THE BIGGEST MOON IN
THE SOLAR SYSTEM!

Between the orbits of Jupiter and Mars is a large asteroid belt. It is occupied by lots of asteroids, which can be very small or as big as small planets.

ARTOO, THE POSSIBILITY OF SUCCESSFULLY NAVIGATING AN ASTEROID FIELD IS—WHAT? OH, WE ALREADY PASSED IT. WONDERFUL!

If an asteroid crashed into a planet, that planet would be changed forever. Some scientists believe that this is how dinosaurs became extinct.

ASTEROIDS

ASTEROIDS CAN BE MADE OF ROCK, METAL, OR EVEN ORGANIC MATTER.

Mars is the Red Planet. Mars is all rock now, but it may once have had rivers, lakes, and oceans.

MARS

LIKE EARTH, MARS HAS SEASONS. POLAR ICE
CAPS ON MARS SHRINK WHEN IT'S WARMER
AND GROW WHEN IT'S COLDER.

This is Earth. Unlike most planets, it can support life. Oxygen in the air and water allow all kinds of people, animals, and other organisms to live there.

IT IS A VERY NICE PLANET, EVEN IF IT IS RATHER SMALL.

EARTH

THERE ARE CURRENTLY ALMOST 7 BILLION PEOPLE LIVING ON EARTH. ABOUT 30% OF THE EARTH'S SURFACE IS COVERED WITH LAND, WHILE 70% IS COVERED BY OCEANS.

Space junk floats around the earth. There are thousands of pieces floating in Earth's orbit. A lot of the junk is satellites, some of which are no longer in use. The ones that still work provide things like cell phone service and cable TV!

IRIDIUM SATELLITE

AIDS COMMUNICATION ON EARTH

HUBBLE SPACE TELESCOPE

HELPS LOOK INTO DEEP SPACE

Temperatures on Earth can range from below 0°F / -18°C to more than 100°F / 38°C. But most planets are either much colder or much hotter than Earth.

URANUS
AVERAGE: -364°F / -220°C

NEPTUNE
AVERAGE: -360°F / -218°C

SATURN
AVERAGE: -308°F / -189°C

JUPITER
AVERAGE: -258°F / -161°C

MARS
AVERAGE: -81°F / -63°C

EARTH
AVERAGE: 59°F / 15°C

MERCURY
AVERAGE: 333°F / 167°C

VENUS
AVERAGE: 867°F / 464°C

This bright planet is Venus. Clouds on Venus trap heat from the sun—making Venus the hottest planet in the solar system!

SURFACE OF VENUS

BEEP-BOOOO.

DON'T WORRY, ARTOO, WE WON'T BE LANDING ON VENUS. THE AIR IS TOXIC, AND THE TEMPERATURES CAN GET AS HIGH AS 900°F—HOT ENOUGH TO MELT METAL!

A "day" is the time it takes a planet to make one full spin, or rotation. On Earth, it takes twenty-four hours. But a day on Mercury is over 1,407 hours long—that's more than fifty-eight days on Earth!

I AM FLUENT IN OVER SIX MILLION FORMS OF COMMUNICATION, BUT THESE FACTS ARE MAKING MY HEAD SPIN!

MERCURY

EVEN THOUGH IT IS THE CLOSEST PLANET TO
THE SUN, TEMPERATURES CAN GET QUITE COLD,
DROPPING TO -279°F / -173°C AT NIGHT.

The star in the center of this solar system is called the sun. The surface of the sun is about 10,000°F / 5,538°C. In the center, it may be 27,000,000°F / 15,000,000°C!

THE SUN IS SO BIG, IT CAN FIT ONE MILLION EARTHS INSIDE OF IT.

IS IT JUST ME, OR IS IT REALLY HOT IN HERE?

BEEP-BOOP-WOOOOO!

THE SUN

THE SUN HAS BURNED FOR 4.5 BILLION YEARS. IN ITS CURRENT STATE IT WILL PROBABLY BURN FOR 5 BILLION YEARS MORE.

The planets we've seen so far move in circles around the sun—these are called orbits. Cooler parts of the sun look darker. They are known as sunspots.

Particles leave the sun and make a solar wind that can travel up to 373 miles per second. Sometimes the particles burst from the sun's surface making a solar flare.

SUNSPOTS

SOLAR FLARE

It's time for our friends to go home—but they'll be back! There's so much to explore in the Milky Way, and in other galaxies far, far away!